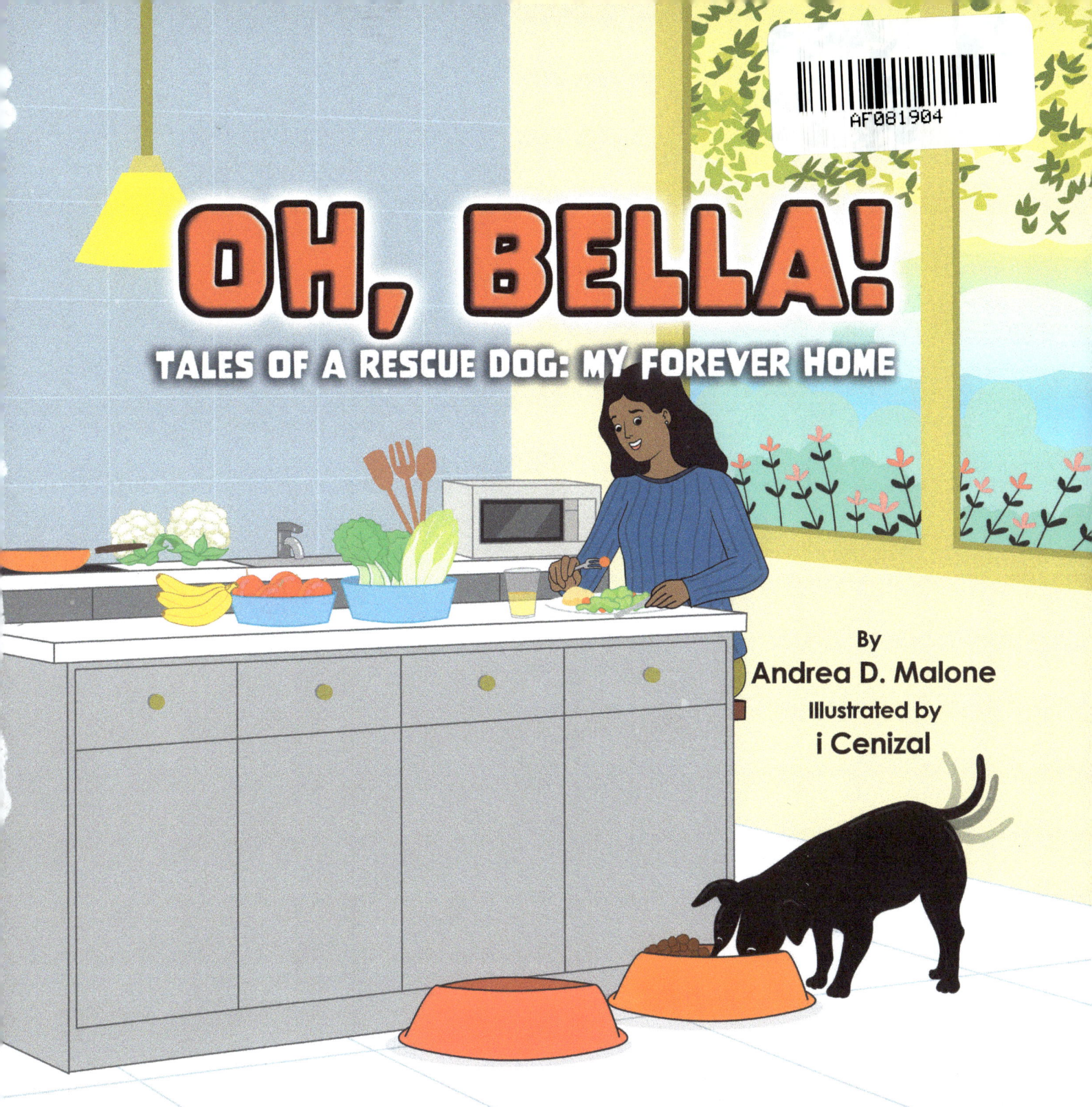

Oh, Bella! Tales of a Rescue Dog
Copyright © 2020 by Andrea D. Malone

All rights reserved. No part of this publication may be reproduced, distributed, or transmitted in any form or by any means, including photocopying, recording, or other electronic or mechanical methods, without the prior written permission of the author, except in the case of brief quotations embodied in critical reviews and certain other non-commercial uses permitted by copyright law.

Tellwell Talent
www.tellwell.ca

ISBN
978-0-2288-3332-1 (Hardcover)
978-0-2288-3331-4 (Paperback)
978-0-2288-3333-8 (eBook)

Dedication

This story is dedicated to the memory of my forever angel, my sweet momma: Juanita A. Malone.

Introduction

In 2015 I adopted my Bella, a Labrador and pit bull mix, from a local animal shelter on her second birthday. I had been looking at dogs at the shelter and couldn't decide which dog would be best for me. After mentioning that they had a dog that would be perfect for me, one of the workers offered to bring her out. At the time, I didn't know Bella was on the 24-hour euthanasia list. Bella had been at the shelter so long! When the worker brought her out to meet me, Bella rolled over for me to give her a belly rub and we formed an instant bond. I had never been a dog owner before, and I knew in my heart I wanted to share my love with a puppy. In this series of books, I want to share my joy of *Oh, Bella! Tales of a Rescue Dog*.

Oh, Bella, let's go upstairs to Mommy's room where you will sleep.

Oh, Bella, this is Mommy's room and here is your soft dog bed.

Oh, Bella, let's get ready for 'night 'night. Mommy is going to take a bath.

Bella likes to keep me company while I'm taking my bath. Bella lays down by the bathtub as I bathe.

Oh, Bella, let's go to bed.

Bella jumps in the big bed with Mommy. Bella and Mommy snuggle up and go 'night 'night.

Good night, Bella, and welcome home! Mommy loves you!

Bella is wagging her tail as she curls up next to me as she sleeps.

Meet Bella...

CPSIA information can be obtained
at www.ICGtesting.com
Printed in the USA
BVHW021748250421
605637BV00012BA/1933